The Bayo

Fast Play Napoleo... ....

for 10 to 15mm Mass Units

2ⁿᵈ Edition

By Cameron H. Frame, April 2022

Photo credit: Battle of Borodino by Louis-François, Baron Lejeune. Public domain. Photo via <a href="https://www.goodfreephotos.com/">Good Free Photos</a>

Introduction

The objective of these rules is to provide a very easy and quick method of undertaking a Napoleonic Wars battle using miniature figures. These rules are written under the assumption that the reader has a basic understanding of Napoleonic era armies, formations and tactics. They attempt in execution to quickly replicate the mechanics and outcome of short, sharp encounters on a limited space battlefield, the table top, without tedious record keeping or ponderous coordinated unit limitations.

I have found over many years of Napoleonic wargaming that simple and fast rules make the game more fun. There are many rules available that, through granular detail can feel like plodding through an accountancy exam rather than spending an enjoyable couple of hours refighting battles in miniature. I've also realized that simplicity of approach does not necessarily lead to a lack of realistic outcomes on the table top.

The main emphasis of these rules therefore is to dispense with calculating firepower accuracy, casualty counts and a myriad of other things that can be included in complicated rules systems and go directly to what is most important; the morale impact that the troops involved in a battle experience. If all else is left out one can boil the essence of the wargame down to three circumstances in which a unit's morale is tested and from that can come three possible outcomes. Everything else can be factored into these circumstances. Morale is tested when troops are receiving enemy fire or receiving enemy charges that make contact and if starting the move in contact with an enemy unit, engaging in a continuing melee. In all of these cases a roll of two dice (2xD6) modified by circumstances adding or subtracting from this total dictate the resulting fate of the unit. It either continues to stand it's ground or becomes shaken/unformed, possibly retreating a little or routs towards the rear. Unit bases are lost when they rout or are run down reflecting a loss of unit strength both physically and morally. In addition, there are rules and restrictions on how units are formed and moved keeping their capabilities within historic context and physically practical reality.

There are no mechanics included for determining more specific casualties, commanders' experience or competence, multi-unit coordination, whether units follow orders or not or the units' national characteristics, a feature that's become so prominent in rules these days. These rules can be modified by the players to introduce such game play aspects however it is suggested that these additional rules are unnecessary given the objective of a fast play battle. It should be noted that any of the rules stated herein may be modified by the reader if deemed necessary to conduct an enjoyable game.

Though these rules were developed for 10mm to 15mm scale miniatures in mind they can just as easily be applied to 25/28mm scale or with dimensions halved for 6mm scale miniatures if base size is less than recommended.

Formations:

Infantry units (battalions) are comprised of generally 3 or 4 bases of figures, Cavalry units (regiments) 2, 3, 4 or 5 bases and artillery batteries any number from 1 to 4 bases (2-8 guns). Skirmishers 1 to 4 bases. Bases are a reflection of a fraction of a larger unit and not a representation of a company or squadron necessarily. The number of figures on each base and the base sizes are up to the individual player. It is recommended that all infantry, skirmisher and cavalry bases be roughly 2 to 2½" frontage and artillery bases be about 1½" frontage. This is only a suggestion. If your existing units have a variance to these dimensions, the rules are flexible as long as both opposing forces have in the most part, similar formation dimensions to each other.

Infantry units form in mobile columns and lines or stationary squares. Columns can be single (march columns) or double base frontage (attack columns). Separate skirmish units are in skirmish order for the duration of the battle. 1 base of formed light infantry is the equivalent of 3 bases of skirmishers.

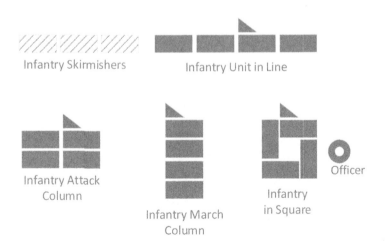

Infantry Skirmishers

Infantry Unit in Line

Infantry Attack Column

Infantry March Column

Infantry in Square

Officer

Figure 1 – Infantry Formations showing bases.

Cavalry units form in mobile columns and lines.

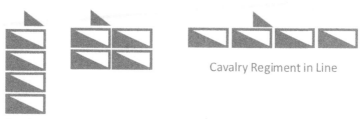

Cavalry Regiment in Columns

Cavalry Regiment in Line

Figure 2 – Cavalry Formations showing bases.

Artillery units are either limbered for movement or unlimbered and stationary.

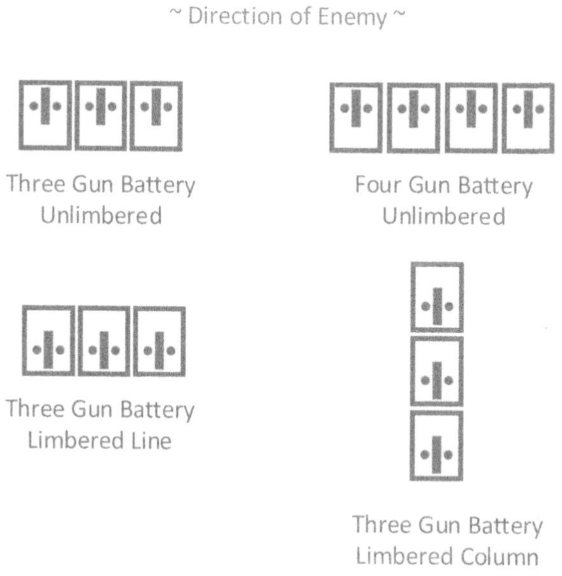

~ Direction of Enemy ~

Three Gun Battery
Unlimbered

Four Gun Battery
Unlimbered

Three Gun Battery
Limbered Line

Three Gun Battery
Limbered Column

Figure 3 – Artillery Formations. Note limbered guns are indicated by their reverse direction.

Artillery men may <u>break formation</u> and shelter inside infantry squares in times of danger if they are within 10" of the square. Once they leave the square they reform in the area they originally evacuated.

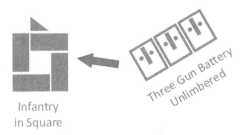

Infantry
in Square

Within 10"

Figure 4 – Artillery may seek shelter in nearby Infantry Square if it is within 10" distance. When they leave the square, they reform in the previous location.

Units in play are either formed or unformed (stressed & shaken).

Units that are shaken/unformed should be represented askew in some fashion on the table top (not in formed straight lines and columns).   Enough so that by a glance one can recognize its status.

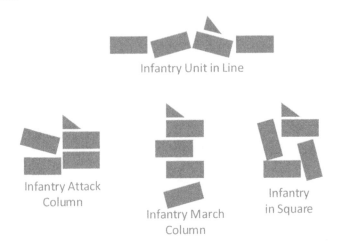

Infantry Unit in Line

Infantry Attack
Column

Infantry March
Column

Infantry
in Square

Figure 5 – Infantry Formations in Shaken/Unformed status.   Note formations are askew so as to easily identify their status.

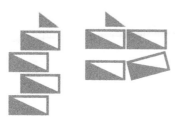

Cavalry Regiment in Line

Cavalry Regiment in Columns

Figure 6 – Cavalry Formations in Shaken/Unformed status. Note formations are askew so as to easily identify their status.

Artillery units are never categorized as shaken/unformed.

For the purposes of firing and melee morale tests, single bases are not considered unformed.

Routing units are in rear facing, shaken/unformed columns.

~ Direction of Enemy ~

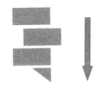

Routing Infantry
in March Column

Figure 7 – Infantry Unit routing toward the rear in Shaken/Unformed status. Note one base has been eliminated during the rout. The unit is facing away from the enemy.

Whole or parts of units may not combine to form new or larger units during the battle except in the case of infantry squares where a maximum of two battalions may form one square as occurred at waterloo and artillery and skirmishers may seek shelter inside. The two battalions must be within 5" of one another. Otherwise all units must remain separate and maintain some separation of physical space between them.

Units may dispatch bases to act independently however these bases are subject to all the morale penalties for being smaller units.

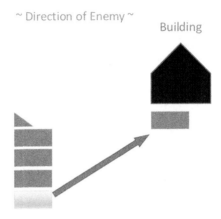

Figure 8 – Infantry Unit has dispatched a base to occupy a nearby building. The rest of the unit carries on with three bases.

If a cavalry regiment splits up during a charge, breaking formation, any multi-base parts still together are considered unformed. Refer to melee rules for further details.

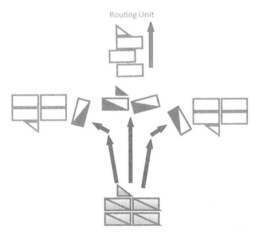

Figure 9 – Cavalry regiment splits up to attack enemy units' flanks and also to pursue routing unit in centre. Note the two Cavalry bases together in centre become unformed after the regiment splits into separate parts.

Units are categorized in three divisions for morale purposes. They are either elite, regular or militia (including Landwehr and Cossacks). If the players choose they can alternately classify their units as Experienced/Veteran, Regular or Raw formations. This would require extra tracking of a unit's status beyond the recognizable uniform differences. Either way the same morale bonuses or penalties should apply.

Scales:

Roughly speaking each turn represents a couple of minutes of real time. Each inch about 10-15 yards. Unit bases, regardless of the number of figures on them, represent between 100 and 150 men. Skirmish bases roughly 33 to 50 men. Artillery bases represent 2 actual guns. Scales are approximate and represent a rough range for the intent of the game.

Start of Game:

Both sides agree on the side to take the first move as the attacker. If agreement is not reached, then each side rolls a die to see who gets the initiative.   Each side might be set up wholly or partially initially on the table with units introduced from the edge of the table top as the game progresses.   Historical engagements may be re-enacted, or new scenarios created. The size and composition of each opposing force is to be determined by the players prior to the start of the game.

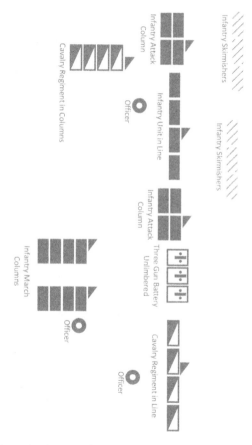

Figure 10 – Example of an army's initial game set-up with all arms and Officers.

Sequence of Turns:

In each turn, one side is designated the attacker and the other the defender. The sides then exchange this status alternating for the remainder of the game.

1. Attacker attempts to rally routing (mandatory) or shaken/unformed units (optional).
2. Attacker Specifies/Declares Orders for each unit if any (move, charge, change formation, fire, retreat, etc).
3. Attacker moves units (units moved can not subsequently fire except for skirmishers and artillery making small adjustment of position 2" or less).
4. Defender fires only where contact has been made from an attacker charging.
5. Attacker units receiving fire roll for morale effect and implement results.
6. Attacker fires or initiates melee where contact is made from a charge this turn or carrying over from a previous turn. Note melee roll by defender will not occur if charging unit is repulsed from defenders' fire.
7. Defender units roll for effect and implements results.
8. Reverse order of attacker and defender and repeat 1 to 7 (keep alternating for duration of battle).

Rallying Units:

Shaken/unformed units may attempt to rally.

Routing units <u>must attempt to rally</u>.

Shaken/unformed units that do not attempt to rally remain shaken/unformed and may carry on as such with all stated restrictions and implications.   A routed or shaken/unformed unit which rallies does not regain any lost bases.

A shaken/unformed unit is considered to still have some essential cohesion and can thus continue to function in limited ways as defined by movement, firing and morale testing rules.

During the rally phase, a Commander can be moved to and attach himself to a unit within 20" distance to assist in rallying the unit (only one unit can be rallied per commander per turn).

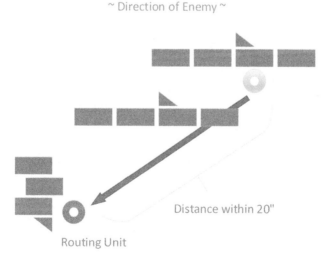

Figure 11 – Officer moves and attaches himself to a routing unit in attempt to rally it. Note the intervening unit is not an obstacle for the officer's movement.

To rally a unit, roll two dice (2xD6).

- Add 2 to total if unit is elite.
- Add 1 to total if unit is cavalry.
- Minus 2 from total if unit is militia/Landwehr/Cossack.
- Minus 1 for each base lost from original unit strength.

Results:

5 and higher with commander attached or 8 and higher if no commander is attached:

- If Routing (backs to enemy), unit will turn around, remain shaken/unformed in any formation and carry on as a shaken/unformed unit.
- If shaken/unformed and facing enemy, unit will rally and form again facing enemy carrying on it's move in its existing formation. For example, a shaken/unformed line will regain it's form as a cohesive line or a column as a column.

4 and lower with commander attached or 7 and lower if no commander is attached:

- Routing unit will continue to rout toward the rear this turn in shaken/unformed column and lose one more base.
- If shaken/unformed and facing enemy, unit will fall back a further 3" still facing the enemy and lose one base.
- Artillery do not fall back and do not become shaken/unformed. They either rout or not.

If a routing unit has no reasonable path around backing units or is within 3" of a backing unit located for the greater part within 45 degrees to the routing units' rear it will cause the backing unit to become shaken/unformed itself with the routing unit fleeing around or through it.

~ Direction of Enemy ~

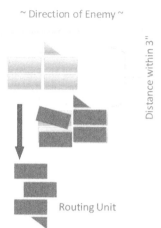

Distance within 3"

Routing Unit

Figure 12 – Lead unit routs, losing a base and moving 8" to rear impacting a rear unit that is within 3" and largely within 45 degrees causing the rear unit to become shaken/unformed. The rear unit however does not move.

Units falling back 3" will cause a rear unit for the greater part within 45 degrees to the falling back units' rear to fall back too if there is no room as both units are still managing to keep a semi-cohesive state to their formations (unlike routing units which are in a state of disintegrating).

~ Direction of Enemy ~

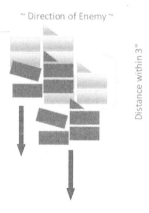

Distance within 3"

Figure 13 – Lead unit falls back 3" shaken/unformed and causes rear unit to also become shaken/unformed and fall back due to it being within 3" distance and largely within 45 degrees of the rear. Both units are attempting to retain cohesion and still face toward the enemy.

Skirmishers routing or falling back do not cause backing units to become shaken/unformed or pushed back. The skirmishers will melt through and around these units.

A unit that continues to rout because of failure to rally does so at this phase and does not move in phase 3. Units that are just shaken/unformed and fall back may still proceed to move in phase 3, change formation or fire.

Routing units must be moving to the rear of the battlefield or if logic dictates, in the opposite direction of the units' major threat such as an enemy unit it just lost a melee to. If they exit the table, they are lost for the remainder of the battle. Friendly units pushed off the table by units falling back are also lost for the remainder of the battle.

Any commander attached to one of these units may detach at any time to subsequently return to the front on his next move.

Each turn a unit routs causes it to lose another base until it is reduced to one base. If the single base routs again from another test brought on by fire or melee, it will be removed from the battlefield.

Movement Rates and Rules:

Infantry in line move up to 6".

Infantry in Column move up to 8" (also routing infantry/skirmisher units will move at this pace in rear facing shaken/unformed columns.

A column may move half way (up to 4") and form a line within enemy infantry firing range however that line will become shaken/unformed until it is rallied.   This movement rule only applies to columns trying to move and rapidly form line within enemy line infantry firing range of 15" otherwise the column must use a whole move to change formation slower but more cohesively.   There are risks in either scenario as would be the case under enemy fire.

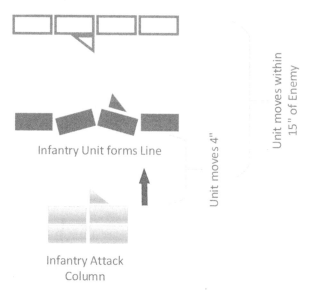

Figure 14 – Column moves forward up to 4" and rapidly changes to unformed line within 15" firing range of enemy unit.   If move and rapid change is not employed, and a full turn is used to form line, the unit will not be unformed at the end of the maneuvering.

Infantry units may move through a friendly artillery battery however it becomes shaken/unformed on the other side. The next turn the unit automatically forms again. In addition, the impacted artillery bases are prohibited from firing due to the movements of the units.

Infantry units may move through friendly skirmishers without becoming shaken/unformed on the other side.

Skirmishers move up to 10" (skirmishers are the only unit that may first move and then fire in the same turn). Skirmishers are always considered to be unformed, but the half move restriction and unformed morale penalty do not apply to them. Skirmish units may retreat without having to change facing (may go backwards) melting around or through other friendly units without penalty and can move full distance in a sideways direction while remaining facing the enemy. They must maintain a distance of at least 3" from enemy units unless they are occupying a building. If enemy infantry or artillery approach them they will back up to a minimum of 3" distance from the enemy. This may push them behind their own backing units. Cavalry on the other hand will overtake them in a charge and melee. See skirmisher melee rules. Skirmish units never cause friendly formed bodies of infantry, cavalry and artillery to become shaken/unformed when they pass through them and vice versa. If a few more inches are required to position the skirmish unit, this is acceptable (they must be scrambling to get out of the way!).

Infantry in square formation can not move, they must expend a turn to change formation to column or line. If they become shaken/unformed they remain where they are and do not fall back 3" the way units do in other circumstances. Squares by their nature do not have a flank or rear facing. If they route they become a rear facing shaken/unformed column fleeing at rout speed. Skirmishers, commanders and artillery may hide in squares (place these up against or inside the square – they can not fire when in squares). If the square routs they rout with the fleeing infantry unit and also lose a base each in the rout.   The minimum required to form square is two bases.

Heavy Cavalry move 12" (also all routing cavalry units will move at this pace in a rear facing shaken/unformed column).

Light Cavalry/Lancers move 14"

All Cavalry charge up to 16" – can be attempted if contact is estimated that it can be made (not measured in advance).   If the unit comes up short and contact is not made from a charge the unit becomes shaken/unformed due to it getting exhausted and less cohesive in the effort.   Cavalry may use a portion of their regular movement allowance to maneuver and face the unit they are charging.   They must charge the opponent within 45 degrees of the cavalry units front at the point that the target has come into direct line of site in a straight line after pivoting /maneuvering.

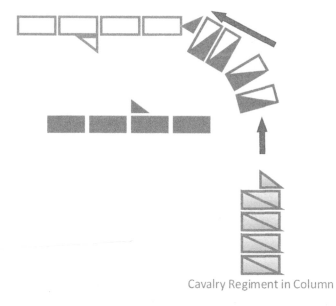

Cavalry Regiment in Column

Figure 15 – Cavalry may maneuver to align their charge against the enemy. All the more reason not to risk forming square too late.

Shaken/unformed cavalry may still charge the enemy however at only half speed, 8".

Cavalry units may move through a friendly artillery battery however it becomes shaken/unformed on the other side. The next turn the unit automatically forms again. In addition, the impacted artillery bases are prohibited from firing due to the movements of the units.

Cavalry units may move through friendly skirmishers without becoming shaken/unformed on the other side and vice versa.

Artillery move at infantry column rate (for foot artillery) 8" or cavalry regular move (for horse artillery) 12" when limbered. Unlimbered artillery can not move any distance except to change facing to their flank which takes one turn. They may about face 180 degrees with no movement or firing penalty. A special move of up to 2" is allowed to each unlimbered battery per turn (attacking player only) to make adjustments to distance forward or backward and or angle and still be able to fire on the same turn. The entire battery front must pivot, not the individual guns. This represents the ability of gunners to rapidly reposition their pieces in the heat of the action to take advantage of developing situations. Artillery may not intentionally unlimber within 5" of formed enemy units unless those enemy units are skirmishers which do not impede artillery.

When artillery rout it is assumed they have rapidly harnessed some of their guns and hauled them away.

All shaken/unformed units move at half rate (except skirmishers). Note, artillery units are never categorized as shaken/unformed though they may be routed at times.

Shaken/unformed units may change formation but remain in a shaken/unformed state (i.e. a shaken/unformed unit can form a square but continues to be categorized as a shaken/unformed unit which subsequently makes it a weak square that is more likely to be broken by a cavalry charge or infantry and artillery fire).

Units that cross a stream or large hedge or low wall become shaken/unformed on the other side (as shaken/unformed units they move at half speed for remainder of their move allowance once over the obstacle). On their next turn they will automatically form again without requiring a rally test. In between they are subject to a morale or firing penalty for being unformed. If a unit has a ford or bridge to cross a river it does not become shaken/unformed on the other side (must be in march column/single base front). Infantry units that occupy wooded areas are considered shaken/unformed. Cavalry and artillery can not occupy wooded areas, buildings or sandpits and cannot cross high walls. Hedges are assumed to be penetrable by all units which would find a way to chop through them. The rules for obstacles on the table top are to be agreed by both players prior to play. For example whether a river feature is passable, if a wall is a high wall or a low wall etc.

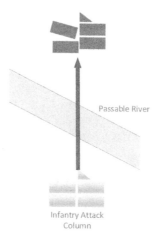

Passable River

Infantry Attack Column

Figure 16 – Unit becomes temporarily unformed after crossing a passable river. The next turn it will automatically form again. Same for low wall or large hedge or if passing through friendly Artillery Battery. Applies to both Infantry and Cavalry. Past the obstacle, unit moves at only half speed for remainder of turn due to it's unformed status.

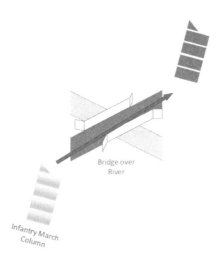

Figure 17 – Unit with single base frontage remains formed on other side after crossing a bridge or ford. Applies to both Infantry and Cavalry.

Infantry formation change takes one move. The unit may change facing at the same time. Part of the unit must occupy the same area as they were in at the start of the formation or facing change.

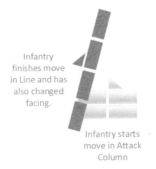

Figure 18 – Units may change formation and facing in the same turn.

Artillery batteries limbering, and unlimbering take half a move (the other half can be used for movement but not firing). They must be limbered to move any significant distance. Routing artillery units (what's left of them) are considered limbered. A special move of up to 2" is allowed to each battery per turn (attacking player only) to make adjustments to distance any direction and or angle and still be able to fire on the same turn. This represents the ability of gunners to rapidly reposition their pieces in the heat of the action.

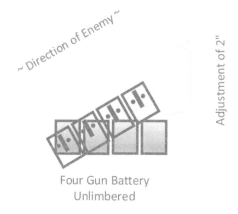

Four Gun Battery
Unlimbered

Figure 19 – Artillery Battery adjusts angle 2". May also move forward or back 2".

Cavalry may change formation and facing (pivot) on the move as long as they do not exceed their movement distance allowance.

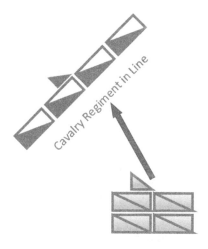

Cavalry Regiment in Column

Figure 20 – Cavalry Units may change formation and facing on the move.

A unit that is engaged in a melee may not change formation or fire except for squares and units in buildings (see firing rules).

A unit that is in melee with an enemy attacking from the rear may turn to face the enemy unit on the next turn (if they are still engaged) when it is designated as the attacker and continue the melee. Units in a continuing melee from the flank will not change facing but can still be the attacker in morale rolls.

Units reversing facing 180 degrees may do so without penalty (ie they may do so once and move in the same turn including to disengage from a melee). Be warned, a unit retreating may get a volley or charge in the back. Units changing face to either side greater than 45 degrees in the same position require one move to do so. Infantry and cavalry may shift sideways at half speed only without having to change facing. Changing face and formation is allowed in the same move.

Buildings: one base of infantry or one unit of skirmishers may occupy a standard building at any given time. When skirmishers are in a building they are considered to be acting as one formed base for firing and morale purposes.

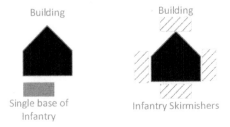

Figure 21 – A single base of formed Infantry or a unit of Skirmishers of 1-4 bases may occupy a building. Place the base(s) up against the side(s) of the building to indicate the building is occupied. The skirmishers are considered to be a formed single base of infantry while they occupy the building.

Commander figures move in straight lines up to 20" and can pass through friendly units with no penalty. They may either be attached to specific units or standing separate. If they have been involved in rallying a unit or attempted to rally a unit they can not subsequently move elsewhere for the rest of the turn but have the choice of remaining either where they are or remaining attached to the rallying/routing unit if the unit subsequently moves.

Formed Infantry and Cavalry units can not deliberately interpenetrate each others' formations.   As per formation and drill instructions of the period, units passing through the same area would form columns to enable and conduct a passing maneuver.   This may occur simultaneously.

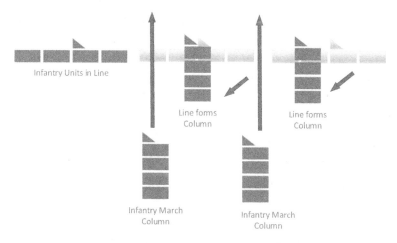

Figure 22 – Units that pass each other will require a formation change in close quarters as per period regulations.   Units may not interpenetrate each other with the exception of skirmishers or units passing through an artillery battery. Note in this example the lines form columns to allow the rear units to advance. Both maneuvers can occur simultaneously.

All units have the capability of moving forward obliquely as long as it is within 45 degrees to the front face of the unit.   If a unit is moving greater than 45 degrees to it's front is must pivot it's facing moving forward and end up with it's facing at an angle to where it started from.   Alternatively, as stated earlier it can use one move to change facing greater than 45 degrees if it remains occupying the same area.

Receiving Fire, Being Charged & Melee (the Morale effect):

For each unit 1) receiving fire or 2) receiving a charge that 'made contact' or 3) units defending in a melee, roll two dice (2xD6) and make adjustments in accordance with the table in Appendix A to determine the impact of these actions. In multiple morale tests by one unit, the worst-case outcome always applies. Note: artillery units are never categorized as shaken/unformed.

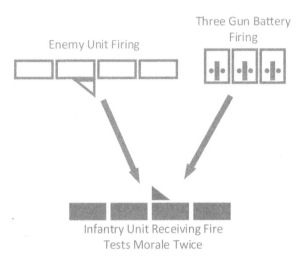

Figure 23 – Morale Test Scenario. A defending Infantry unit has come under fire from an attacking enemy Infantry Line and an Artillery Battery. Both sources of fire are to be tested separately by the Infantry unit with the worse case result, if any, applied.

All firing takes place after units are moved. The point at which the morale test is taken is the farthest point the unit has <u>potentially</u> moved to. Falling back or routing is measured from this point.

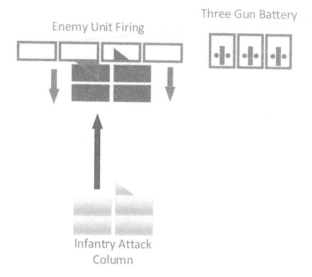

Figure 24 – Morale Test Scenario. An attacking Infantry unit has advanced against a defending enemy line with the aim to make contact and melee. The Infantry unit is moved up to it's furthest potential distance and as this brings it into contact, it will receive fire from the enemy line. At this point it will test morale for coming under close range defender fire and any falling back or routing will be measured from this point. Note the artillery battery was not contacted and so will not be a source of a morale test, it being allowed to fire when it is either contacted directly or when it is it's turn as the attacking player.

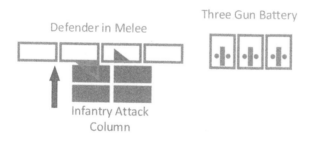

Figure 25 – Morale Test Scenario. An attacking Infantry unit has successfully passed its morale test for being under fire and is now in contact with the defender unit. The defender unit will now have to take its own morale test being the defender in a melee. If the defender passes its morale test then both sides remain in contact for the next move with the defender becoming the attacker on the next turn.

Musketry and rifle fire are effective up to 15" from any point of the firing unit.   Artillery fire is effective at ranges from 0 to 10" for close range, 10" to 30" for long range and 30" to 60" for extreme range.   Targets must be within 45 degrees of the front of the firing unit.   Though the weaponry can fire further, it is not effective enough for a morale test to be taken and can thus be ignored for game play.

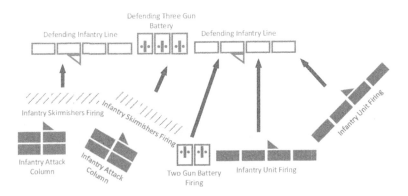

Figure 26 – Morale Test Scenario.   Each arrow represents a morale test required of the defending players units.   Note the Defender unit on the right side is under tremendous pressure requiring it to test three times on the same turn.   The worst-case scenario will apply.   The attack columns on the left side can not fire as the skirmishers are in the way.

Units on the reverse slope of hills can not be fired on.   They can only be fired on from the upper part of the hill (contour) or from level ground beside the hill.   Line of sight is always required. Artillery may fire from hilltop across and over a valley to another hilltop over any in between formations.   Units may fire uphill or downhill.   Artillery units on an elevated level firing downhill may only fire over friendly troops on a lower level if these friendly units are within 10" of the firing battery.   Those friendly units further then 10" from the elevated artillery are considered too close to a level plain or to the enemy that they may receive friendly fire – in the back!

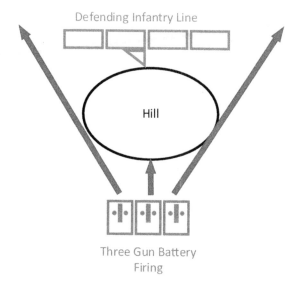

Defending Infantry Line

Hill

Three Gun Battery
Firing

Figure 27 – Morale Test Scenario. The attackers Artillery Battery can not fire on the defender behind the hill due to lack of line of site. If the defender was on the hill, the attacking artillery would be able to fire on it.

Units receiving a charge in their flank with contact 45 degrees or less of their front can not fire into the attacking unit.

Units in melee may receive fire in flank or rear from other nearby enemy units.

Units in melee that cause the opposing force(s) to fall back or rout will occupy the space vacated but will not come into further contact with an enemy unit on the same turn. They must stop just short of contact by at least ½". The exception is when cavalry run over skirmishers – they will continue their charge and subsequently may receive fire and melee with a unit beyond the skirmish line.   Refer to skirmish melee rules for further details. Cavalry involved in melee with artillery must stop at the artillery position due to the jousting occurring around the guns and carriages.

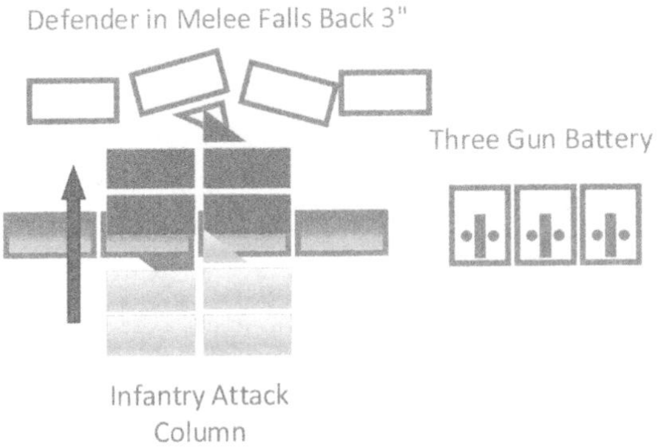

Defender in Melee Falls Back 3"

Three Gun Battery

Infantry Attack Column

Figure 28 – Morale Test Scenario.   The defender has failed it's morale test and falls back 3".   The attacking unit will follow up and occupy the area vacated by the defender but will remain at least ½" from the enemy unit.

Infantry and artillery, unless involved in counter battery fire or combined battery fire, must target their fire on the enemy unit in closest proximity to them (excluding skirmishers which can be ignored if they are not the target) and can fire up to 45 degrees to their front. If multiple targets are estimated to be the same distance from the firing unit, it may select which target to fire on.

If the closest enemy unit to skirmishers firing are skirmishers themselves then these must be the target and not formed bodies beyond the skirmish line.

Only the front-rank bases if infantry and artillery can fire.   Range is determined by the closest edge of base to edge of base measurement between the firing unit and the target unit.   Line of site is required. If the line of site is for the most part obstructed by a friendly unit then firing is not allowed.

Firing is always counted as coming from the entire units front-rank.   Remember, this reflects the morale impact on the target and is not an attempt to reproduce accurate and detailed firing scenarios.   The targets morale is what is being measured.

Any fire from cavalry is not considered to be significant enough to warrant a morale test and is thus ignored.

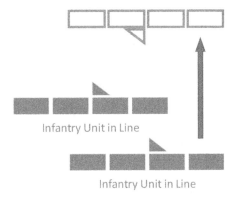

Figure 29 – The rear unit, being for the most part obstructed by a friendly unit in front, is prohibited from firing at the enemy even though a portion is visible.

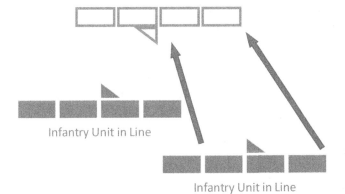

Figure 30 – The rear unit, being for the most part not obstructed by the friendly unit in front, is allowed to fire at the enemy with the majority of the firing unit in line of sight of the enemy. Defenders morale test is based on all four attacking bases firing.

If skirmishers are caught between an enemy unit firing and its main target at artillery close range (up to 10") or infantry any range (up to 15"), they will roll for coming under fire as well by the entire battery or infantry formation. Skirmishers, unless they are the target do not need to roll for morale effect from long and extreme range artillery.

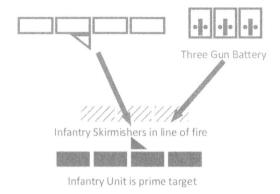

Three Gun Battery

Infantry Skirmishers in line of fire

Infantry Unit is prime target

Figure 31 – Skirmishers screening a unit coming under fire will also have their morale separately tested in addition to the prime target.

Infantry units and artillery can not fire through their own skirmishers – these must be moved away first (only the attacking force may move their skirmishers proactively).

Units will only fire once per turn except when receiving charges that make contact from multiple units in the same turn. See following example.

Each incident of receiving fire or a charge is rolled separately. If two infantry columns assault an infantry line or an artillery battery, the entire line or artillery battery will fire full volleys at both columns separately and roll for receiving a charge from each column that makes contact separately. If both columns become shaken/unformed and fall back 3" or rout because of defender fire, then contact is not considered to have been made and the defending line does not have to roll for receiving the charge. An engagement may potentially require rolling multiple times in one turn. Similarly, if one cavalry unit is charged by two opposite cavalry units there will be dice rolls (2xD6) resulting from each unit making contact with the worst-case outcome applied.

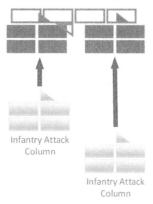

Figure 32 – Two Infantry columns assault an enemy unit in line. Both attacking columns will each take a morale test for being fired on by the entire defenders' line. The columns will be moved up to contact the enemy unit before the morale test is rolled. Any routing or falling back is measured from here.

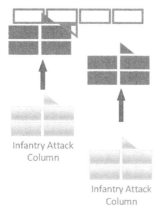

Figure 33 – Two Infantry columns assault an enemy unit in line. In this case the left side column reaches the enemy line and will have to test morale for receiving enemy fire. The right side column moves the full distance of 8" but does not reach the enemy line and will not test morale for receiving enemy fire.

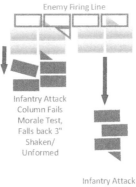

Enemy Firing Line

Infantry Attack
Column Fails
Morale Test,
Falls back 3"
Shaken/
Unformed

Infantry Attack
Column Fails
Morale Test
Routing 8" and
Loses a Base

Figure 34 – Two Infantry columns assault an enemy unit in line. In this case both attacking columns failed their morale test caused by enemy fire. One unit has routed losing a base, the other unit falls back 3" (should be interpreted as failing to reach enemy line in the first place, halting 3" from enemy). Falling back and routing is measured from the furthest point the columns potentially moved to.

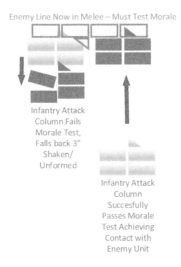

Enemy Line Now in Melee – Must Test Morale

Infantry Attack
Column Fails
Morale Test,
Falls back 3"
Shaken/
Unformed

Infantry Attack
Column
Succesfully
Passes Morale
Test Achieving
Contact with
Enemy Unit

Figure 35 – Two Infantry columns assault an enemy unit in line. The left side column fails its morale test and does not make contact. The right side column however passes its morale test and is in contact with the enemy line. The enemy line will now have to test morale for being the defender in a melee.

Artillery firing at extreme range 30" – 60" must first roll 1xD6 and achieve a 6 to cause the target to take a morale test.   If a 6 is rolled then the target tests for morale using the same method testing for long range 10" – 30" or per counter battery fire for long range 10" – 30".   If the die roll is 1 to 5 then the artillery fire has been ineffective or missed the mark.

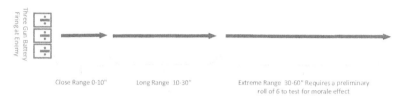

Close Range 0-10"   Long Range 10-30"   Extreme Range 30-60" Requires a preliminary roll of 6 to test for morale effect

Figure 36 – Artillery Battery firing ranges.   Extreme range requires an additional preliminary roll of 6 to determine if a target is hit, causing a morale test.

Cavalry units (regiments) may voluntarily become unformed by splitting up and attacking targets of opportunity with one or more bases.   From this point when the "squadrons" are split off attacking various enemy units, they will have morale impacts of being smaller units in melee and may be subject to being fired on by defending enemy units.   As they are now testing morale as separate units, a single base that routs is removed from the game.   An example of this splitting up is if a cavalry regiment of four bases finds itself breaking an infantry unit in line, the subsequent move there may be open enemy flanks to either side – a base may split off and pivot and attack the exposed flanks on either side while the remainder proceed to follow and harass the routing infantry.   At some point either on the spot or if there is a general retreat these "squadrons" may come back into a shaken/unformed formation again.   This situation may also occur as cavalry regiments swarm around a series of infantry squares.   Any multi-base parts of a split regiment are considered unformed.

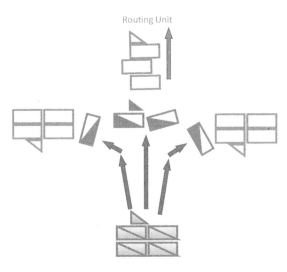

Routing Unit

Figure 37 – Cavalry regiment splits up to attack enemy units' flanks and also to pursue routing unit in centre. Note the two Cavalry bases together in centre become unformed after the regiment splits into separate parts.

If enemy units start the move already in contact face to face and the attacker does not choose to break off, turn and retreat, they are considered in melee and may not fire from the front of the unit (an exception is made for a unit in square or in buildings in melee on one side which may still fire from other sides). The defender in a melee will roll in effort to resolve the melee same as receiving a charge.

A unit that is in melee with an enemy attacking from the rear may turn to face the enemy unit on the next turn when it is designated as the attacker and continue the melee. Units in melee from the flank will not change facing but can still be the attacker in morale rolls.

An infantry unit that occupies a building (one base) is treated similar to a unit in square formation when it comes to firing and melee. If it is charged and in melee from one or more sides it may still be able to fire out of the other sides of the building(s) not so engaged (even though it is only a single base). Only other infantry may assault infantry in buildings. Cavalry may not do so, and artillery and skirmishers can only fire at the occupants of the buildings. Skirmish units may occupy and defend an empty building and do not have to automatically retreat in the face of nearby enemy units the way they do in the open. In this instance they are to be treated as though they are one formed base. A single base within a building is able to fire out of any or each side counting as a single base in each resulting morale test.

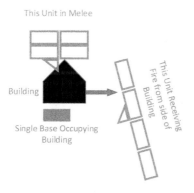

Figure 38 – A single base occupying a building is simultaneously in melee with a unit on one side while conducting fire (as a single base) at an enemy unit from another side of the building.

An enemy envelopment is defined as a unit being in contact from the front and from the rear at the same time except when it is cavalry attacking an infantry square or infantry attacking a building. A melee situation which involves enemy envelopment will cause a unit to immediately rout without rolling dice. This special circumstance will cause the entire unit to be immediately removed from the battle instead of just a single base. It is a rare circumstance, but it does occasionally happen.

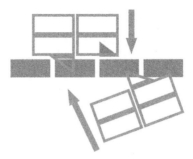

Figure 39 – If a unit is caught in a melee from the front and rear at the same time it will be eliminated, and all bases immediately removed from the table.

Squares comprising of two bases are rectangular and can not fire from the narrow ends, there not being enough muskets to make a difference however that narrow side is treated like any other in melee (not as a flank).

When a unit has been reduced to a single base it stops routing and turns to face the enemy. It is no longer considered shaken/unformed and represents the final hard core of the unit that has stuck together (for its own safety). It will move at column speed if infantry or regular speed if cavalry. If infantry, it is not large enough to form an effective square. If it routs again due to another morale test the base will be removed from the battlefield.

Skirmishers in Melee:

Skirmishers are generally run down and eliminated when charged by cavalry being unable to outrun them. In this case one base of skirmishers are eliminated for each base of cavalry that come into contact with them as an <u>entire unit</u> (there is an off chance that the skirmish fire will throw back the cavalry before contact can be made).   If any skirmisher bases remain after the unit is run down, they will test morale as per normal melee resolution and potentially escape by falling back or routing.   The cavalry will extend their charge to the maximum distance beyond the skirmishers that were run down and this may bring them into contact with another enemy unit subsequently receiving fire again and possibly conduct a further melee. Measure out the full cavalry distance charge before any dice rolls. Note this is the only circumstance where a charge may be measured out in advance.

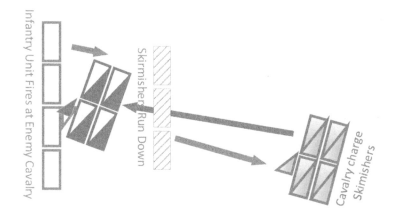

Figure 40 – Diagram illustrates how a Skirmish line can be run down by Cavalry if Skirmish fire fails to halt the Cavalry charge. In this case the Cavalry will charge their full distance past the Skirmishers' line, eliminating them and may run into a backing enemy unit which will fire on them causing a further morale test. If the Cavalry pass this morale test as well, then the Infantry line is required to test morale for being in melee with the Cavalry.

Skirmishers will not be involved in melee with enemy infantry or artillery bodies. If they are approached by the enemy infantry or artillery, they will retire to a distance a minimum 3" from and facing the enemy even if it is not their turn to move. If this pushes the skirmishers back into a friendly unit, they do not make it shaken/unformed but will instead move around the unit to its side or through it to the other side. If a few more inches are required to position the skirmish unit, this is acceptable (they must be scrambling to get out of the way!). Skirmishers can not charge the enemy including other skirmishers or artillery however they may move as close as 3" from the enemy but never closer.

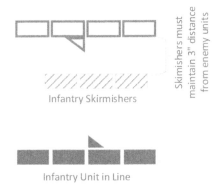

Figure 41 – Skirmishers must maintain a distance of at least 3" from enemy lines. If enemy advances the skirmishers will fall back keeping at least 3" away except when occupying buildings or sheltering in an Infantry square.

Skirmishers that join in a square for protection are not factored in the size of the formation or add to it's firing capacity.

Skirmishers (1 to 4 bases) that occupy a building are considered to be one formed base until they are ejected or leave the building at which time they resume their skirmish formation.

Artillery in Melee:

Artillery are generally eliminated when charged by cavalry or infantry once contact is made.   In this case one base of artillery is eliminated for each base of cavalry or infantry that come into contact with them as a whole unit. There is a good chance that the artillery fire will throw back the attacking enemy before contact can be made unless they've been assaulted from the flank or rear.   If any artillery bases remain after the unit is involved in the melee, they will test morale as per normal melee resolution and potentially escape by routing.   The attacking unit will stop at the location of the artillery unit occupying the ground the artillery unit was in.

Counter Battery Fire:

Artillery may target enemy artillery specifically in an effort to reduce or eliminate it.   To conduct counter battery fire, each gun firing will roll 3 dice (3xD6) at long range from between 10" and 30", requiring a roll of three of the same number to score a hit and eliminate one enemy gun.   The odds of this occurring is 2.78% per gun firing.

Counter battery fire at extreme range 30"- 60" requires a preliminary roll of 6 on (1XD6) to score a chance to roll a hit as per long range 10" to 30".   First achieve a roll or 6 with one die and then roll 3 dice requiring a roll of three of the same number to score a hit and eliminate one enemy gun.

In short range of 0" to 10", only 2 dice (2xD6) need to be rolled with each double achieved removing one enemy gun.   The odds of this occurring are 16.7% for each gun firing.

Enfilade: if counterbattery fire is directed at the flank within 45 degrees at any range up to 30", only 2 dice (2xD6) need to be rolled with each double achieved removing one enemy gun.   For extreme range a preliminary roll of 6 (1xD6) is required before a possible hit can be rolled with 2 dice (2xD6) as per the above.

Artillery targeted by counter battery fire are <u>not required</u> to take a morale test.

Coordinated Battery Fire:

Multiple artillery batteries that are within 10" of each other may coordinate their fire on a single target. For example, three batteries are coordinating fire being 10" between battery 1 and 2 and 10" between battery 2 and 3 or 20" total or less. The target in this case does not have to be the closest enemy unit. This coordinated fire results in a devastating impact to the dice roll as the number of guns are counted for the targets morale roll. The maximum number of guns that can be combined for one roll is 8. Guns in combined batteries in addition to 8 will have their target rolled separately and for lesser effect. For example, 9 guns fire at long range; the first 8 guns will cause a morale penalty of -4 to the target. The 9th gun will fire, and morale will be rolled separately with a penalty of 0 per Appendix A table. The 9th gun must be targeted at the same enemy unit that the combined batteries are firing at.

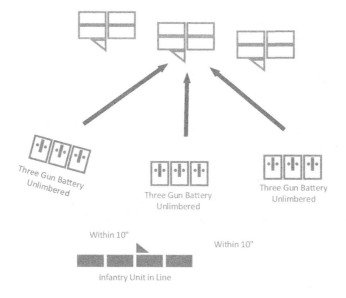

Figure 42 – Coordinated Artillery fire by nearby Batteries within 10" can target a specific enemy unit up to a maximum of 8 guns. 9th gun in this case also fires at same target but rolls separately and to lesser effect. Artillery range is what the majority of the guns can achieve.

Officer Casualties:

Each attacking players' officers in phase 4 will roll 3 dice (3xD6). A total of 18 (3xd6) or 0.46%, will kill the officer and he is removed from the game as a casualty. It is assumed stray fire is occurring and individual crack shots from units are undertaking sniping activity at all times.

An officer caught in the path of an enemy cavalry charge or attached to a unit wiped out will be removed as a casualty. They can not be the intended target of the charge however, just in the way at the wrong place at the wrong time.

Results of Dice Rolls with Adjustments:

0-4: unit routs, loses one base, becomes shaken/unformed, takes march column shape facing away from enemy, immediately retreats 8" if infantry or foot artillery, 12" if cavalry or horse artillery. (see rallying and move instructions for additional rules). Units in buildings will rout as any other unit routing. Any friendly units in the path of a routing unit will become shaken/unformed (but remaining in situ) with the routing unit going around and behind. This may involve slightly further distance than rout distance to position the units which is acceptable. All formations are subject to routing and base losses.

5-6: cavalry or infantry units become shaken/unformed, facing enemy, falling back 3" (unless infantry is in square which remains in situ). Any friendly units in the path of a falling back unit will be pushed back themselves in a shaken/unformed unit retaining its basic formation except artillery and skirmishers which remain in situ with the falling back unit going to it's rear. This may involve slightly further distance than falling back speed to position the units which is acceptable.

If unit is already shaken/unformed it remains so, falling back 3".

Skirmishers (already unformed) fall back 3" but do not cause rear units to become shaken/unformed.

Artillery units are never categorized as shaken/unformed and never fall back unless they are routed.

Units in buildings will fall back 3" as any other unit falling back, evacuating the building and moving toward the rear.

7+ unit continues as is, standing its ground whether shaken/unformed or not.

Note: routing and falling back take place immediately once a unit has failed its dice roll. This may impact other actions already set in motion such as a second enemy unit charging or firing at the same target. These secondary situations will need to be logically thought through in regard to if further action is required.   For example, if a unit is both fired upon and charged in flank and routs from the first dice roll, the second dice roll is not required as the worst-case scenario has already been realized. If a unit is required to undertake a morale roll more then once, the most severe outcome always applies. i.e.: routing will take place over falling back or carrying on.

All rolling for situations is assumed to be simultaneous.   If a unit moved while fully formed and then subsequently becomes shaken/unformed, a unit adjacent to it also testing morale still gets the morale bonus of having a nearby formed unit. It's shaken/unformed status is effective once all testing for the round is complete. This is important to keep in mind as the presence of a nearby formed friendly unit can make the morale difference of whether a unit breaks and routs or not.

Additional Notes on Rule Play Concepts:

The table top is a relatively small area on which to conduct operations. The typical table used is imagined to be your dining room table or something of that size. The time envisaged for a game, "the battle" is the equivalent of probably half an hour or slightly more of real time when fully played out. Battles of greater length would involve a greater size table and/or miniature armies that nearly no one can replicate unless you use miniature units to represent whole brigades or divisions. That is not the intent of these rules which stick to a battalion/regiment level depending on if you are referring to infantry or cavalry.

Rolling dice to determine an outcome is a necessary thing to bring into the conflict an imponderable factor of chance which would occur in real life. There are many factors that can influence the outcome of this chance and these are applied to the roll in a mathematical sequence to bring us to a more likely outcome. What makes an attack fail? What makes one succeed? What causes one unit to be brave and another to crumble? There is always a degree of chance involved which makes the game unpredictable, winnable or defeat possible. Good tactics should prevail such as concentrating fire or resources at a weak point but there's always a chance that things can go awry. The dice partially give us the answer.

Though movement and firing is staggered in game play, alternating between attacker and defender, one must imagine everything taking place in a fluid series of events and this staggered morale testing is just a moment in time amongst this fluidity where events potentially pivot in one direction or another. This is the best practical way to resolve developing situations in reproducing Napoleonic battlefield mechanics on the table top with miniature figures.

Bases represent large bodies of men with casualties not calculated specifically. Casualties are assumed to be happening with each episode of firing and melee and if sizable, results in a unit routing or falling back losing bases (men) as they do so. It is assumed that if the target unit has failed it's morale test from enemy fire, it has likely incurred significant casualties. As well losing bases from failed rallying and routing represents not just casualties but also soldiers fleeing the action, surrendering to the enemy and a unit's overall morale attrition. For example, if 25% of an army's bases are lost that represents casualties, morale attrition, prisoners and of men leaving the units on the battlefield adding up to 25%.

Firing is an abstract concept representing a cumulative effect that does not necessarily occur as a single volley. Units testing morale for receiving fire are testing for all fire coming from a single source. Each source firing causes a new morale test to be rolled and calculated. The act of a unit coming under fire may actually represent several volleys inflicted upon it in one turn by a single source. The morale test represents all fire received from a specific source over a period of time (the turn) and geographical distance travelled. For example, an infantry column approaching an infantry line may in reality receive 2 or 3 volleys before coming to blows. This is why the test is made at the farthest movement the column potentially achieved that turn and the result may be that the column routs/retreats or halts a short distance from the enemy, becoming shaken/unformed.   Another test may be for artillery firing into the columns' flank. This again is rolled separately being a different and an additional stress the column is under.   In real life columns rarely achieved contact with a well formed firing line at close range.   This was demonstrated over and over again in the Peninsular war and at Waterloo.

Attack columns of 2 base frontage are encouraged as the preferred formation for infantry assaulting enemy lines in these rules through a morale bonus of 1 and an accelerated pace of 8" as opposed to the slower movement of formed lines at 6" and no morale bonus for a march column of 1 base frontage. This reflects historical reality. In the right circumstances, an elite unit in attack column with a command figure attached, screened by skirmishers and with a formed supporting unit nearby within 5" has a morale bonus of 6 making it formidable indeed and hard to stop.

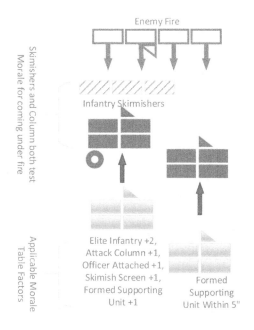

Figure 43 – Maximum morale effect – Elite/Guard unit in column facing enemy infantry with officer attached, skirmish screen and formed supporting unit. Other morale factors will be negatives for firing range, contours and number of bases firing. The forward formed unit on left side will draw enemy fire being the closest target.

In these rules' infantry forming square to repel cavalry require an order to do so. This reflects reality. All formation changes and unit actions require officers' orders. Woe to those that delay in forming square or have the hubris to stand firm deliberately in line to face enemy cavalry. If their musket fire does not stop the enemy cavalry charge, there is a significant morale penalty for getting into melee with cavalry when not in square.

Counter battery fire is generally discouraged by the rules through its low probability of success. It is nonetheless an option, especially at close range. Historically counter battery fire was not very effective and mostly avoided being considered a significant waste of ammunition.

There is no overall command apparatus in these rules. As a player you assume the command decisions for each unit as if you were its individual commander or the commander in higher ranks controlling the whole affair. Commander figures on the table top are considered senior and influential enough to be used to rally routing and shaken units as needed or attaching themselves to forward units for a morale boost. A lack of a command figure in an area of the battlefield will quickly show in the various units' ability to retain cohesion under pressure. There is no rule for the number of command figures used. This can be agreed between the players. It is suggested that the ratio of command figures to units deployed is no greater then 1:2 and more likely 1:3 or 1:4. Command figures could represent anything from a major to a field marshal and are not specifically differentiated from each other.

Battles are fought until there is an agreed upon winner. Players should agree on winning conditions for each side at the start of the game. For example, the capture of a hill or the successful defence of the hill or crossroads. The loss of a certain number of units off the battlefield or the lose of a certain percentage of overall bases (recommended at not exceeding 40% of the army's total bases including artillery and skirmish bases). Remember base lose represents not just casualties but also soldiers surrendering or fleeing the field / melting away from the action, ineffective, present but no longer with their unit.

The concept of a unit falling back 3" is not literal and represents not necessarily any physical contact followed by a retreat. It may represent falling back / running away or it may represent a failure of a unit to reach a target psychologically, slowing down and physically halting 3" from the enemy and losing some cohesion /

losing nerve due to the stress on it's morale which has been impacted by many factors.   Falling back is a range of reactions captured in one phrase and rule to reflect a unit's failure under stress to stand it's ground or reach its target.

The term melee is used when determining morale impacts of units potentially coming into hand to hand contact. If a defender is contacted by an attacker and fails it's morale test it can be interpreted as losing the brief hand to hand combat or it can also be interpreted as the defender losing it's nerve and retreating or even routing before contact is actually even made. The emphasis here is on the morale of the units involved and resolutions can be accounted for in more than one way. All that maters is the results of the morale testing of the units involved. Historically many charges did not end up in hand to hand combat at all but rather one side or the other fleeing the pending carnage expected from a determined enemy, especially one that could not be halted by the defenders fire. This is especially true in cavalry encounters where there was significant back and forth.

Specific scenarios are built into the rules. For example, the French often resorted to the tactic of advancing in column to face the enemy and rapidly deploying into a firing line at the last minute. In these rules this rapid advancement and formation change within enemy fire range will cause the unit to become unformed and thus more vulnerable then usual and less able to fire effectively.   An accompanying commander should be able to successfully roll to rally the unit to form again and it can proceed to fire in strength. If not, it will fire in a less effective shaken status and is more likely to remain shaken and pushed back as happened in many historical instances, the most famous being the last advance of the French guard at Waterloo. Units that take more time to move forward and deliberately change formation the next turn risk further exposure to enemy fire. The quick attempt to form line has its advantages and disadvantages.

Cavalry may charge enemy infantry and artillery face on however the resulting fire received will very likely be devastating to the charging cavalry. Cavalry perform best when able to pivot on the move and outflank the enemy. Even in this case, the target may have nearby supporting units that can fire into the flanks of the cavalry. This is best demonstrated by a series of infantry squares firing from all angles in support of each other. Cavalry exposed to such fire into it's flank and rear will not last long before retreating. In these rules it is nearly impossible for cavalry to break a formed square. If the square however has become shaken/unformed then it's chances of a successful charge increases. So bring up that horse artillery to support the attack.

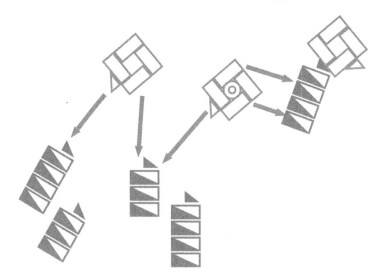

Figure 44 – Illustration of attacking players' Infantry Squares firing on nearby Cavalry. Each arrow indicates a separate morale test that must be conducted by the targeted Cavalry formations with the exception of the two arrows coming from the same square to the same target on the right which counts as two bases firing once into the enemy flank.

The amount of volleys and their impact on the battlefield reflect the reality that units rarely came into physical contact / melee. Most units will lose their nerve before physical contact is ever made and the factors featured in the morale table along with dice roll probabilities reflect this reality.

For simplicity of game mechanics, all artillery batteries are generalized in effectiveness, rates of fire and range.   All artillery was deadly at close range and less effective at longer range and inflicted a similar degree of terror and carnage amongst its targets regardless of calibre.   Artillery by its nature is not easily shaken and so will stand it's ground unless it is entirely routed in which case it will lose strength (abandoned or destroyed guns).

The shaken/unformed status of units represents a state of stress between a solidly firm unit and a routing, retreating, fleeing unit. It is a status that represents a unit's unwillingness to full heartedly follow orders, be less formed, more disorganized, less effective at volley fire and harder to control only moving at half speed in a less coherent formation.   It represents a weak moment when disturbed by negotiation of obstacles in the field be it a thick hedge, traversing a wall, woods, sand pit, moving through a friendly artillery battery, etc.   It is psychologically half way between willing to fight and wanting to flee.

The high morale penalties for defending in a melee reflect the shock of a unit unable to halt an enemy with volley fire and the likelihood of a sudden immediate resolution to the melee.   The momentum and initiative are with the attacking unit at first.   If the melee continues, the initiative and momentum swing to the other side which has now become the attacker on the next turn. If a unit gets enveloped, it is a goner.

Skirmishers in these rules have limited effect in small numbers. They may occasionally score a success at close range. When screening a unit they provide a morale bonus which may be their greatest benefit. If deployed incorrectly they could hinder a firing line. The timing for their withdrawal can be critical when the need comes for a battalion in line to respond to an attacking column. Skirmishing riflemen firing are more effective then regular light infantry. The idea of separate skirmish units deployed for the duration of the game reflects the reality that when armies are deployed at this close range (the table top) those designated to perform in a skirmishing function have already been ordered to do so and are being sent forward. Unless they are occupying a building, these skirmish formations remain in skirmish order for the remainder of the battle.

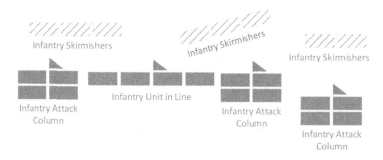

Figure 45 – Skirmish screen deployed. Note that all four formed battalions are considered screened. If any part of the skirmish bases cover the line of fire to a rear unit, the rear unit is considered screened receiving a morale bonus of +1.

Routing units are masses of retreating men who have partially disbursed around and off the field of battle or cavalry with winded or wounded horses. On the given day of battle, they can not be counted on anymore while they are still routing. These men in reality would congregate, reform and be collected again in the evening and the days after the battle.

It is highly recommended that gameplay is cooperative, and no one tries to game the rules by measuring to the quarter inch if a unit is in firing range or not or if fire is truly directed at the flank rather then the front of an enemy unit. In the case of firing or attacking in flank, remember the physical representation of the depth of units represented by miniature figures is distorted. Look carefully at the 45 degree angle and whether it's likely that a flank hit is truly and obviously achieved. If there is a dispute it must be close; roll a die each (1xD6) to see who wins the argument of front vs flank.   The intent of the rules is for simple play with whole units firing or in melee.   Movement should be taking place realistically.   Fair play and a degree of graciousness leads to the enjoyment of all.

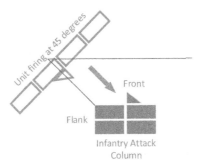

Figure 46 – Firing on Flank. If a unit is firing pretty exact on 45 degrees at it's target, it should be considered to be firing at the front of the enemy unit due to the distortion that miniature figures give to unit representations.   If in doubt or dispute, each player can roll a die to decide if fire is at flank or front with the die roll deciding the argument.

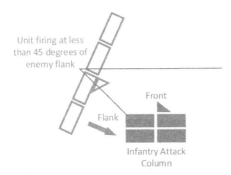

Figure 47 – Firing on Flank. If a unit is firing at an angle less than 45 degrees to the targets front, then the target is considered to be receiving fire in it's flank. This will have a significant impact to its morale test. In this case there should be no doubt or dispute.   Even though only a portion of the unit is firing at the flank the morale test will be based on the entire line firing at the flank.

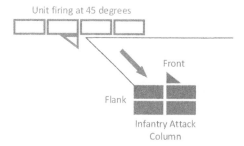

Figure 48 – Firing on Flank. In the above scenario, again the factor of distortion that miniature figures give to unit representations argues that the target unit should test morale for receiving fire from the front and not the flank.

Optional Rules:

Troop Quality: More variation can be given to morale bonuses and penalties for elite and militia type units.   For example, Prussian Landwehr in 1815 was almost as good as the line units and so can have a morale penalty of -1 instead of -2.   French Old and Middle Guard could have a morale bonus of +3.   Russian and Austrian composite line grenadier battalions can have a bonus of +1 being better than the average line unit but not quite on the level of a guard unit.

National Characteristics: Can be introduced into the morale table for some nations that were notorious for being unreliable. Spanish, Neapolitan and Turkish units can all be subject to -1 morale penalty in all tests.   Some may argue that the British/Scottish units should have a morale bonus of +1 (though I disagree) being highly trained.   It is up to the players to agree.

Formations: Restrictions on formation use by some nations can be introduced for certain time periods.   Some people believe the British should be prohibited from using attack column formations though I myself disagree with this.   It was accounted for in the training manuals and its lack of use was more a command decision than any inability to muster and use the formation. Other restrictions on the attack column can be given to the 1806 and earlier Prussian infantry, 1807 and earlier Austrians and Russians as well.

General Panic: test the morale of any unit within 5" of a friendly routing unit specifically to determine if it routs too.   Give these nearby units a -1 in their morale tests as their spirits would be falling seeing the nearby routing unit.   This could conceivably cause a big gap in your battle line if one routing unit causes others to rout too.

Coordinated Battery Fire: Coordinated battery fire must be directed at the closest target.

Appendix A: Morale Testing Table for Receiving Fire or Melee Contact

Adjust total roll of two dice (2xD6) as follows:

Unit formed	0 (no adjustment)
Unit shaken/unformed (not including skirmishers & single bases) or:	-2
Unit is routing	-4
Unit has commander attached to it	+1
Unit is Elite/Guard	+2
Unit is Militia/Landwehr/Cossack	-2
Infantry in line under long or extreme range artillery fire	+1
Infantry in attack column formation with two base frontage (except when under artillery fire)	+1
Infantry screened by own skirmishers within 15"	+1
Unit in defended position (buildings/fortification)	+3
Unit in defended position (walls/sand pit)	+2
Unit in defended position (woods/large hedge)	+1
Unit has a friendly formed unit within 5" (at start of all unit's morale testing)	+1
Unit is on lower ground than opposite it is interacting with	-2
Unit receiving infantry fire from 0-5"	-3 (-4 for rifles firing)
Unit receiving infantry fire from 5-10"	-1 (-2 for rifles firing)
Unit receiving infantry fire from 11-15"	+1 (0 for rifles firing)
Unit under fire from only one base of infantry (ie side of square, building or column front)	+3
Unit under fire from only two bases of infantry (ie two sides of square or double column front)	+2
Unit receiving skirmisher fire or fire from shaken/unformed infantry	+3
Unit receiving fire or charge in flank (45 degrees) or rear	-3
Unit receiving fire is in skirmish formation	+2

Unit under close artillery fire 0-10"	-1 (for every base of artillery firing)
Unit under long range artillery fire 11-30"	-1 (for every 2 bases of artillery firing). 0 for 1 base firing
Unit is infantry in square (not if unit is under artillery fire or is in a fortified position/building/wall/woods etc or in melee with enemy infantry)	+3
Infantry unit is charged/in melee by cavalry & not in square	-5
Unit in melee is a single base against a larger unit (except when single base is behind walls or in buildings)	-2
Units in melee against single base (except when single base is behind walls or in buildings)	+2
Cavalry in melee with infantry not in square	+4
Light cavalry except lancers in melee with heavy cavalry or lancers	-2
Heavy cavalry/lancers in melee with light cavalry	+2
Infantry in melee with other infantry unit of same size or larger in open ground. Cavalry in melee with other Cavalry unit of same size or larger in open ground.	-3
Infantry in melee with other infantry unit of smaller size in open ground. Cavalry in melee with other Cavalry unit of smaller size in open ground.	-1

Receiving Fire, Being Charged & Melee (the Morale effect):

Roll 2xD6. Make adjustment per Appendix A.
0-4:   unit routs, loses one base, becomes shaken/unformed, takes column shape facing away from enemy.
5-6:   cavalry or infantry units become shaken/unformed, facing enemy, falling back 3". (unless infantry is in square which remains in situ). If unit is already shaken/unformed it remains so, falling back 3".
7+   unit continues as is, standing its ground whether shaken/unformed or not.

Appendix B: Quick Reference Sheets

Turn Sequence:

1   Attacker attempts to rally routing (mandatory) or shaken/unformed units (optional)
2   Attacker Specifies/Declares Orders for each unit if any (move, charge, change formation, fire, retreat, etc)
3   Attacker moves units (units moved can not subsequently fire except for skirmishers and artillery making small adjustment of position 2" or less)
4   Defender fires only where contact has been made from an attacker charging
5   Attacker units receiving fire roll for effect and implement results
6   Attacker fires or initiates melee where contact is made from a charge this turn or carrying over from a previous turn.   Note melee roll by defender will not occur if charging unit is repulsed from defenders' fire.
7   Defender units roll for effect and implements results
8   Reverse order of attacker and defender and repeat 1 to 7 (keep alternating for duration of battle).

Rally:

Roll 2xD6.

- Add 2 to total if unit is elite.
- Add 1 to total if unit is cavalry.
- Minus 2 from total if unit is militia/Landwehr/Cossack.
- Minus 1 for each base lost from original strength.

5 and higher with commander attached (8 and higher if no commander is attached):

- If Routing, unit will turn around shaken/unformed in any formation and carry on as a shaken/unformed unit.
- If shaken/unformed and facing enemy, unit will rally and form again facing enemy carrying on it's move in its existing formation.

4 and lower with commander attached (7 and lower if no commander is attached):

- Routing unit will continue to rout this turn in shaken/unformed column and lose one more base.
- If shaken/unformed and facing enemy, unit will fall back a further 3" still facing the enemy and losing one base.   Artillery do not fall back and do not become shaken/unformed.

Movement Rates:

- Shaken/unformed units move at half rate (except skirmishers).
- Units negotiating obstacles become shaken/unformed until next turn.
- A special move of up to 2" is allowed to each artillery battery per turn (attacking player only) to make adjustments to distance and or angle and still be able to fire on the same turn.
- Units reversing facing 180 degrees may do so without penalty.
- Infantry in line move up to 6".
- Infantry in Column move up to 8" (also routing infantry/skirmisher units will move at this pace in rear facing shaken/unformed columns).
- A column may move half way (up to 4") and form a line within enemy infantry firing range however that line will become shaken/unformed until it is rallied.
- Skirmishers move up to 10" (skirmishers are the only unit that may move and fire in the same turn).
- Units may change formation and facing on the same turn.
- Infantry in square formation can not move. If they become shaken/unformed they remain where they are and do not fall back 3" the way units do in other circumstances.
- Heavy Cavalry move 12" (also all routing cavalry units will move at this pace in a rear facing shaken/unformed column where space allows).
- Light Cavalry/Lancers move 14"
- All Cavalry charge up to 16", Cavalry may use a portion of their movement allowance to maneuver and face the unit they are charging.
- Artillery move at infantry column rate (for foot artillery) 8" or cavalry regular move (for horse artillery) 12" when limbered.
- Commanders move 20"

Counter Battery Fire:

- Roll 3xD6. at long range from between 10" and 30", roll of three of the same number to score a hit and eliminate one enemy gun.
- Roll 1xD6 for a 6 to achieve extreme range hit. For each hit at extreme range 30"- 60" use same method as above.
- Roll 2XD6 at short range of 0" to 10", each double achieved removes one enemy gun.
- Artillery targeted by counter battery fire are not required to take a morale test.
- Enfilade: if counterbattery fire is directed at the flank within 45 degrees at any range up to 30", only 2 dice (2xD6) need to be rolled with each double achieved removing one enemy gun. Roll 1xD6 for a 6 to achieve extreme range potential hit. For each hit at extreme range 30"- 60" use same method as above.

Coordinated Battery Fire:

- Batteries within 10" of each other may combine to target a single enemy unit.   Maximum 8 guns.

Officer Casualties:

- Each attacking players officers in phase 4 will roll 3 dice (3xD6).   A total of 18 (3xd6) will kill the officer.
- An officer caught in the path of an enemy cavalry charge or attached to a unit wiped out will be removed as a casualty.

Appendix C: Dice Roll Probability:

Odds of 'two dice' (2xD6) rolls and likelihood of achieving a minimum rolled result (cumulative %).

Dice	Individual %	Cumulative %
2	2.8	100.0
3	5.6	97.2
4	8.3	91.7
5	11.1	83.3
6	13.9	72.2
7	16.7	58.3
8	13.9	41.7
9	11.1	27.8
10	8.3	16.7
11	5.6	8.3
12	2.8	2.8

Printed in Great Britain
by Amazon

85192071R00037